MASTER AND DISCIPLE:

Morocco's Authoritarianism or the Other Face of Islam

Abdelilah Bouasria

Bloomington, IN  Milton Keynes, UK

authorHOUSE®

AuthorHouse™
1663 Liberty Drive, Suite 200
Bloomington, IN 47403
www.authorhouse.com
Phone: 1-800-839-8640

AuthorHouse™ UK Ltd.
500 Avebury Boulevard
Central Milton Keynes, MK9 2BE
www.authorhouse.co.uk
Phone: 08001974150

First published by AuthorHouse 11/14/2006

ISBN: 978-1-4259-7238-7 (sc)

Library of Congress Control Number: 2006909593

Printed in the United States of America
Bloomington, Indiana

This book is printed on acid-free paper.

To my parents whose love allowed me to grow

To my sister whose kindness pushed me to glow

To my uncle Farid who met his Lord with a shining smile on the face

To Mohamed Choukri Whose influence on Bukowski one can trace

To Sidi Hamza whose light is piercing for the heart

To Big whose rap speaks truth to the fans of art

To Roma, the land of my awakened dreams

To Myriam, the holy lady with all her streams

Contents

A response to Hammoudi's book
Master and Disciple

"And I began to question everything around me: the houses, the shop signs, the clouds in the sky, and the engravings in the library, asking them to tell me not their superficial story but another, deeper story, which they surely were hiding but finally would reveal thanks to the principle of mystic resemblances."

Foucault's Pendulum
Umberto Eco

One of the positive insights in Hammoudi's symbolic exploration of the master/disciple framework is a reintroduction of culture in Moroccan politics. It is obvious, as many scholars would argue, that his book on power, *Master and Disciple: The Cultural Foundations of Moroccan Authoritarianism* is not a paradigmatic shift, given the generous participation of his previous teachers in the delicate yet beneficial task of "going after" power in every corner of the Moroccan map. Hammoudi is among Moroccan pioneers who dared to renounce the class-driven analysis that had permeated the intellectual scene from the Cold War's dawn till its dusk. It is interesting here to notice that in Morocco a student is more likely to learn about Michel Foucault at the department of literature than in the corridors of *political science*, which is a Moroccan euphemism for *legal studies*. Other than a reflection of this rigid wall between disciplines (or a way of controlling discourse according to Foucault), the fact that Foucault is present in Moroccan literature and absent in political science is quite revealing when one sees how mundane literature is in the Moroccan hierarchy of epistemological fields. Bearing in mind that Foucault and power are Siamese twins, we can interpret this academic space of contention (literature as an exclusive field of Foucault, hence of power) as a desire to shift the locus of power to a field that has practically no value in Moroccan society, let alone among its business elite. By associating Foucault and literature, the drawer of curricular boundaries consciously or unconsciously is seeking the following change: Literature will become a locus of power by receiving Foucault in its abode or Foucault would lose its importance once made a citizen of literature. Since the former is still foreign to the Moroccan mind, I tend to espouse the latter. It is in light of this reasoning that I salute the work of Abdellah

Hammoudi, in which he managed to give Foucault his due respect by using his heritage where it hurts the most: the political arena. Many politicians and scholars would probably dislike him for the same reason.

If I had to put a badge on Hammoudi's academic denomination, I would safely use that of cultural politics. Numerous are the scholars who studied the role of culture in the design of political webs, starting from Samuel Huntington at a macro level up to Barthes at a micro level (with his work on signs), without forgetting the interesting symbiotic work of Geertz and Gellner. Every author writes from a social and personal reality, no matter how he or she seems to deny it. Most often do so without being aware of it. Hence, once Hammoudi's book leaves the corporate world of printing, the door is open for sympathizers, deconstructionists, and undecided readers to spot incoherence, magic, and inconsistency in his discourse. Others will seize the opportunity to engage in a marketing exposition of their own school of thought. There are those who will dislike the mere denominational definition of Hammoudi as an anthropologist, suddenly shifting their attack to the discipline of anthropology rather than his actual work. Classical Marxists might condemn him for not using class as a working device, and rational choice theorists will regret the absence of any "operationalization" of his variables if they ever succeed in finding them. Others will look for information about his personal life such as his leniency toward the Moroccan left or his friendly relation with Prince Moulay Hicham, who is a royal figure portrayed by Moroccan media as a sensationalist or a "red" troublemaker in total defiance of the Moroccan constitution demanding respect for members of the royal family[1].

Their critique here leads them to conspiracy theory to show how Hammoudi's account is a mere plot of the "jealous American" mind to provoke "sedition" or *fitna*. Others will celebrate his "new" analysis of power relations not because they are admiring the beautiful construct of the Moroccan anthropologist, but rather because this construct happens to de-legitimize one of their ferocious enemies according to their reading (or misreading) of Hammoudi. Those who are at odds with the Moroccan monarchy— our Republicans, as I like to call them—will overemphasize Hammoudi's critique of the monarchical elite in the same way that those who dislike Sufism will look for every attack on this beautiful Moroccan legacy to adopt it as a mantra. Sufism is the esoteric branch within Islam that deals with heart purification and

4

character perfection following a model named *the master* whom disciples or seekers try to emulate. My point here is that every comment in Hammoudi's analysis of power relations, and my analysis of his analysis, is also satiated with power. Exaggerations and bursts of anger might find their way in the process of this academic debate. Even this point does not gather the consensus of its readers. Those who believe in shock therapy might see anger as a mark of sincerity and a step toward learning. Meanwhile, those who prefer to see the cup as half full rather than half empty interpret this anger as an eternal sign of arrogance and violence, though most often it is a *counter-violence* because controversial knowledge fields constitute a medicine for one another. Where do I find myself in all this?

As is the fashion in anthropological essays, the writer starts with a confession wherein he exposes his background as an addendum to the text he or she produces. Hence, I will expose parts of my life in order to enable the reader to be in touch with the living epistemological "ecosystem" of this essay. A mind that is not familiar with non-modern ways of thinking will be riddled by the nonlinear concept of causality used between my reading of Hammoudi's book, and my only advice is that patience is definitely a virtue of the primitive age. Many points that seem irrelevant or superfluous will be clarified later since our analytical framework is systemic. Many transitions that seem absent are only invisible and our use of transitions cannot but be antagonistic to the empiricist and flashy way of showing transitions. To demand a direct and redundant exposition of transitions between paragraphs is analogous to the fact of inserting in a comedy the line "you should laugh now." However, out of respect for the methodological orientalism governing my "ecosystem," I will try my best to polish my transitions between paragraphs so that they become shining.

God or nature wanted me to see light in this world in the capital of Morocco one night in the middle of the '70s. I was somehow conditioned to wear the turban of that culture in the sense that my tongue had to twist itself in Arabic. (Unfortunately my mother could not teach me Berber.) And my index had to point itself to the *Kaaba* five times a day after my forehead (a symbol of knowledge?) touched the ground as a reminder of the humble origin of my existence: clay. Destiny wanted me to be in the "sample" of Hammoudi's experimental group, which could mean that I lack the capacity to *disassociate* myself from this object of inquiry, but it might also mean that I am engaged in a *praxis*, allowing me to *live* what Hammoudi *knows*. I never saw myself as a scholar and this is probably the reason I never attended any graduation ceremony out of my deep belief in the precepts of Hammoudi's school: cultural symbolism. I follow things to their roots (not to say that I always look for fundamentals), and for me the ritualistic gathering of the graduation ceremonies is a profound and deep act of worship. According to mystics, the spiritual master gives his or her disciple a mantle and a cap to transmit his or her blessing but also to announce that this disciple is now ready to speak in his or her name. Since one cannot have two hearts, I can safely say that I had worn my mantle and cap before I even came to this world and my only endeavor is to keep myself pure enough to preserve this outfit. Thus, I have my own blinders and my personal imperfections that can strip my analysis of the typical calmness with which it is generally adorned, but I welcome warmly those who give me my own shortcomings as a gift, because they are indeed helping me to preserve my mantle. I owe them a thankful recognition and I shall forcefully put them in the chain of knowledge that quenches my thirst as I am gradually transcending toward what is real. If it occurs to the mind of the readers that *real* is used here in its positivistic sense, let them know that it will be a trick of their modernist paradigms since my *real* stands for the divine and not for what is touched or seen.

Because I am not a scholar, I do not have an *audience*; nor do I speak *for a community2*. This is an important point behind my choice of sarcasm and irony (and they are both legitimate figures of speech) to expel my feelings. When I am assured that I am not writing for an audience, I permit myself to engage in a playful game of biting sarcasm because I have the certainty that the buffoon in my plays is no one but me, and had I had an iota of doubt about a potential target of my satirical bullets being sarcasm-proof, I would have pushed my writing ship to sail on dry land. I am rebelling against a past life that I wished to conduct differently, or maybe I am probably just re-channeling my *excess of testosterone* to a more artistic container in case only marriage seems to turn the wolf inside me into an acquiescent sheep. I might as well be tired of being defined as the "other" by the "normalization" of this rape of identity. If I am not called Middle Eastern (Middle to whom?), I am named North African (North to whom?), and if I am ever to be praised it is because of my ability to appreciate techno music and my proficiency wearing jeans and quoting Jay Leno. Carl W. Ernst, a scholar of religious studies, translates the way I feel ignored into an academic conclusion when he notices that *"the term 'Near East' which is the primary designator for Orientalist departments today, was coined by a British naval historian in the period before World War I. Likewise, 'Middle East' is a term invented by the OSS (precursor to the CIA) during World War II, and it had its main applicability during the Cold War."*[3] The theoretical dessert that we get from this short biography is of a dual nature. My practical engagement on a path *legitimizes* my counterargument to Hammoudi as a viewer from the inside, and my resentment of graduation ceremonies is a personal way of saying that the condemnation of primitive rituals in the study of the "savage" is absurd when the "modern" is extremely loaded with the same rituals aesthetically beautified by a marketing arsenal. Hammoudi takes the role of a Western anthropologist condemning the rituals of his backward countrymen when he ties the idea of submission to authoritarianism to the rituals of initiation in Sufi brotherhoods in Morocco. I reserve myself the right then to explore the ritualistic unspoken parts of the modernist project present in the graduation ceremonies.

I did not engage in this clerical confession out of a desire to *sell* myself, for it had already been established that I was not looking for an audience in a world where the veil between *customers* and *audiences* is very transparent. It is my own way of vaccinating whoever comes to my world against any viruses that I might carry with me from the deepest confines of that backward region called the *underdeveloped* world. I am used to confessions in my country, so it does not bother me this time to go over the same exercise, with the slight difference that I am not *forced* to do so (should I revisit my concept of force?). I hope that those who bring their caller ID to their academy (in order to know who is calling beforehand so that they can *pick up the phone* or let it kill itself ringing) will know that I belong to the political culture school with a faith in postmodernism, Sufism, and leftist tendencies (whatever that means) with a serious allergy to diplomacy and false idols. *My "chemical reaction" to Hammoudi's analysis stems from my own faith*, and needless to say, this short sentence contains the *plan* of my work—or shall I call it *a key*? In a less elliptical tone, the sentence mentioned above means that there will be three big aspects to my critique of Hammoudi: a Sufi internal model, a postmodernist re-correction of his design, and a leftist exploration of the author's bias toward the academic right. Anthropology will be seen here as a conservative mouth that leaves the trace of its red lipstick on Hammoudi's neck. The reader will discover this idea mainly in the section where I mention departments and academic exclusions: the reasons I label anthropology as "right" (at least the "anthropology" that the author is representing). But no matter how rational and justified this choice seems to be, power's rigorous gaze will definitely be one explanation.

Hammoudi's book basically relies on two major assumptions:

1) The Moroccan "dictatorship" in the political arena is rooted in the cultural climate of brotherhoods (*Zawiyas*) that use submission of the disciple to his spiritual master. Furthermore, Hammoudi tried to convince us that the legitimacy conferred to the divine was challenged only by sainthood. Against those who will tell us that this point is not capital in Hammoudi's thesis we will quote the Amazon.com editorial review of his book[4]. It goes as follows: "*Building on the work of Foucault, Hammoudi argues that at the heart of Moroccan culture lies a paradigm of authority that juxtaposes absolute authority against absolute submission.*"

2) By serving his master through cooking and caring (called *khidma*, meaning service), the disciple performs **feminine** tasks and therefore the whole master-disciple framework is about loss of power manifest

as "feminization" and loss of manhood. When the disciple becomes a master there is an **inversion** in the process in the sense that the former disciple is the "new dictator" of the path. In order to make sure that our own fantasies are not joining this summary, let the Amazon.com editorial review balance our view. Hammoudi *"contends that as long as the Master-Disciple dialectic remains the dominant paradigm of power relations, male authoritarianism will prevail as the dominant political form."*

Hammoudi invites us to avoid the separation of disciplines by looking at unpredictable sites of power (etymologically the *Zawiya* means corner) through the use of symbolism in dealing with cultural events. In that task, he is certainly walking in the footsteps of Geertz and Gellner and this is where the Sufi that I am awakens. I would use an internal Sufi model to provide an alternative explanation of the master-disciple relationship famous not only among the Sufis but also among all those pre- or anti-enlightenment traditions (Buddhism, Kabala, and Christianity). I will rely on this explanation on an integrated methodology (*manhaj takamuli*) borrowed from the work of a Moroccan philosopher of language (Taha Abderrahmane) whose work will be analyzed later.

The postmodernist part of my self feels jealous whenever an undeserving hand tries to touch the gates of the postmodernist castle. The person I happen to love after God the prophet, my spiritual master, and my parents is Michel Foucault, and this is why I refuse any abuse of the French genealogical work or an inadequate use of his theories. Hence, I will show how Hammoudi betrays the spirit of Foucault when he analyzes the gender aspect of the master-disciple framework or when he underscores the avenues of resistance to power in his account of the feminization of the disciple understood as absence of virility. One might wisely object here that Foucault can be read in different ways according to the teachings of postmodernism. My response to that argument is that it commits the fallacy of contradicting its own essence. If one goes along with the postmodernist condemnation of unique readings of texts, why isn't the assumption that postmodernist hermeneutics reading Machiavelli as Angel Gabriel in itself challenged? In other words, postmodernism abhors unique readings of texts because of their absoluteness, yet it forbids any loathing of this absolutist relativism. Henry Munson says it in better terms when he comments on events interpreted differently by people as *"not invented ex nihilo every time they are interpreted, and to say they have no coherence or meaning of their own is ludicrous, as are the related notions that all interpretations are equally plausible and equally fictional.*"⁵As a reaction to this fallacy I enjoy my right to read Foucault with some freedom of interpretation and with no essentialism, mainly talking about the gender omission of his account of power.

My same postmodernist inclination will lead me to see power relations not only in the master-disciple framework but also in the model used by Hammoudi to assess the master-disciple "reality." Munson elaborates more on cognitive dissonance by taking as a target the "king" of postmodernists, Richard Rorty, when he asks the following question: "*Would Rorty seriously suggest that an interpretation of Plato's Republic by a renowned scholar of classical Greek philosophy and one by a semiliterate high school student were simply two equivalent turns of the hermeneutic wheel?*"⁶ I agree with Munson when he negates the necessity of an egalitarian view of discourses, but I do not see the relationship as unidirectional. The scholar of classical Greece might learn things from the semiliterate high school student in the same way that he teaches him or her other things. This view stems particularly from the perception that God is the ultimate teacher of every soul and that other people, be they carpenters or beggars, are milestones that this ultimate teacher put in our knowledge quest to guide us to the written share of knowledge that had already been allocated for us.

Finally the leftist part of my personality would question the bourgeois nature of the tools used by Hammoudi when analyzing the link between authoritarianism and mystical brotherhoods. An important question would be asked here: In what field of study would we classify this book? Providing an answer to this question is already an inauguration of a power play. Most people will answer that the book is anthropological. Why would they do so? Most of the time, it is because the author is said to belong to a certain discipline and, therefore, his work will tend to be seen within the canons of his discipline. This answer would entail a definition of anthropology. I have this terrible default of jaywalking disciplinary boundaries and questioning departmental exclusions, if not exclusivities. After all, Hammoudi shows clearly how the mystics might produce a better person but they fail to give birth to a good politician.

In this part, I will not be looking at the model that Hammoudi uses or the one that he omits, but I will be showing how power is hidden in the coat of the discipline to which the book pertains. If we choose anthropology, then it is helpful to look for the power dynamics that might be inherent to the field in order to see how likely they are to travel with the author in his symbolic ejaculation. Assuming that Hammoudi was inspired by Geertz and Gellner, it would be interesting here to test the critique made of Geertz by Mark Woodward and Henry Munson by seeing if Geertz is still getting it wrong in the framework of the master and disciple. Insights about the Oriental's assumptions of anthropology as a field will help us unravel the "authoritarianism of the field." One can note here that there is a double erasure of local narratives by the postcolonial mind through an obsession with an often imagined sexual difference and a colonial othering. If we choose education, then it is relevant to show how Hammoudi ends up favoring *institutional* knowledge by waging war on oral forms of transmission of knowledge, a result that I do not feel Hammoudi wanted to achieve. I would show here how alternative forms of knowledge serve best the formation of good politicians.

Let me start my operation by giving it a name and by showing my weapons at the beginning. Let me call this Operation Noble Being (recalling that the American government called its rescue operation after the World Trade Center tragedy Noble Eagle, and ironically enough symbolism falls short when it comes to explaining the origin of the eagle). My weapons are my hypotheses since I chose to take the inductive reasoning road:

Hammoudi is an anthropologist belonging to the school of political culture.

Hammoudi uses Foucault to see whether the relationship of a disciple to a spiritual master explains the authoritarian political system in Morocco.

Foucault is soaked in authoritarianism according to Nancy Fraser, who called him a "Young Conservative."[7]

Hammoudi is neither faithful to the essence of Foucault in his analysis of feminization nor in his omission of the Islamic religious explanations.

Political culture as defined by Geertz and Hammoudi is also soaked in power according to Munson and Woodward.

Anthropology as a field is still suffering from orientalism.

It is possible that the authoritarian tendencies of the Moroccan political system stem from anthropology, political culture or Foucault. With all those *empowered* tools, Hammoudi will find authoritarianism no matter where he tests his hypotheses, whether it is in a nudist beach in Greece, a terrorist camp in Afghanistan or a board of trustees at an American school. When the only tool that a person has is a hammer, everything else will look like a nail. One might say, of course, that I am just reinventing the idea that power is everywhere and I agree wholly with that, but I wonder why the same power that is everywhere is seldom if ever seen with the same eye by people on Capitol Hill or in Hollywood. I do not deny that my eyes are more ready to see power in the Oval Office than in my own town and it is for two reasons. *Power in my town* had received substantial attention from donors, media pundits, and scholars, while *my town without power* is still *relatively* unexplored; *the Oval Office* had received much attention from the same people, but *power in the Oval Office* is still a taboo. There are two reasons for this inequality. First, donors, media, and to a lesser degree scholars choose to remain only on one side. Second, those who manage to cross the line lose their identity as scholars and they are baptized as radicals or propagandists or donors whose money ends up alleviating some superpower's budget deficit when it is not hibernating in a luxurious casino. It is because I like scholars, the media, and donors to preserve their identities that I take it upon myself passionately to stop this unjust treatment.

Hammoudi comes into picture here because he continues to perpetuate this fantasy of the Orient that consists of imagining dictatorship nowhere but in *our backyard*, and had he written a book about the Masonic origin of the American presidential legacy as *still* running the "democratic show," he would have faced many hurdles. First, there is a big probability that he would be deprived of his comfortable chair at Princeton. Second, an anti-Semitist or reductionist would be what people would be calling him. Third, many (and fortunately not all) of those agencies willing to contribute financially to the "discovery of truth" would suddenly become aware of their overzealous generosity and would end up espousing monetary misery as a mode of life.

A) Anthropology and Hammoudi: Is Authoritarianism in Our Heads?

One point that we will be touching upon in this part is that we strongly feel a "racist" dichotomy in anthropological methodology. Let us show this point by asking two questions. Which departments specialize in American politics? Which departments specialize in "non-American" (or in Bush's dichotomy: "terrorist") politics? The answer to the first question would certainly give us a department like government, political science, or public affairs that is heavily funded by Congress or the State. The variables that this department forces on its "disciples" are legislatures, judiciary, Congress, and public opinion. The answer to the second question is area studies, comparative politics, anthropology, and ethnology. And those departments are barely surviving due to poor funding if they do not disappear under the cracking bite of some administrative bodies at the top of the pyramidal university, whose salaries could make a money worshipper faint.

The variables that we find in this second category are witchcraft, religion, theft, Ali Baba, veils, cuisine, and circumcision. There is a terrible dichotomy that is being felt here between law and chaos or civilization and savagery. It is the same divide that realism has constructed a long time ago between order and anarchy. The human imagination has no limit, but PhD dissertation topics dealing with American politics have to be supervised from "*within this department,*" carrying the financial and ideological imprints of their benefactors. Generally, those topics are expected to be about order and civilized intelligent beings: tolerance in American policy making, the dinosaurs are dead and the 'rally behind the flag thesis is still alive, the exemplary independence of the judiciary.

Now let us see the side of the underdeveloped "area" zones where the image of the bare naked and poor slave is very common. Theses have to come from "*within these departments*" and titles run somehow along the following lines: The "Absent Clitoris" in Ghana's Politics, Witchcraft: A New Variable in Development Theory?, and Voodoo Dance Enters Haiti's Court. There is a clear yet un-bridged gap between those two camps. Categorizations and icons are prepared for those who dare to cross the lines. We will summarize this idea in the table below to show how methodology and unquestioned assumptions are often silenced to give way to a totally disconnected reading of the "aboriginal journal." Hammoudi's analysis of the master-disciple is certainly drinking from the breast of such a discipline and I totally agree with those who level at me the charge of falling in the trap of setting a new dichotomy, but my answer to them is that I am against Hammoudi's dichotomy and not against dichotomies in general. (My postmodern conversion is not yet complete.)

What if an area studies approach were used in studying US politics? Typical Titles for Theses

Clinton's Semen: A Blow to U.S. Liberty?

The Not-So-Rational Symbols on the Dollar: Freemasonry and the Religious Roots of American Authoritarianism

Gary Condit and Chandra Levy:
When Rallying Behind the Convict Becomes Rallying Behind the Condit

Fanatics Do Not Booze Before They Blow Up:
Media with a Low IQ and a Huge Purse

VCRs and Big Macs: A Sleeping Public Opinion

The Office of Homeland Security: The Rise of American Fascism

Astrologer Joan Quigley: When a Witch Masterminds Reagan's Détente

Tell Me How You Laugh and I Will Tell How You Govern:
A Correlation Between Clinton's Body Language and His "Dovish" Policy

Gender Apartheid on the Hill: Why our President is Not A Lesbian

The Cuban American National Foundation and
The U.S. Government: Together We Kill!

The Washingtonian Ghetto and Roads:
When You Live in a Glass House You Should Not Throw Stones

Psychics on the CIA's Payroll: Where Does Rational Choice Theory Fit In?

They Gemocracy: Bribery in American Academia

Marc Rich or the *Almost Corrupt* Executive Office

You Can Think Critically But Never Outside the Matrix: When American Colleges Persuade Their Students to Internalize Submission

How U.S politics scholars would call you names

Reductionism

Anti-Semitism

Irresponsible Deviation

Failure to See the Evidence

Communist Tendencies

Islamic Fundamentalism

Conspiracy Theories

Correlation Is Not Causality

Tree Hugger

Shallow and Unscientific Propaganda

What if rational non-oriental titles show up in area studies?

Empirics of the Median Voter Hypothesis in Sudan

Hassan II Called a Former Dissident Who Was Looking
for his Head to Lead His Government: A lesson of Forgiveness

When Moroccan Girls Swing Their Hips in Wedding Dances They
Are Not Attracting a Male Gaze but Are Saying How They Are *first ladies*

The Opposition Newspapers Feed from the Breast of
Big Brother and Still Criticize Him: Have You Said "Censorship"?

The Secret Deal Between the U.S. and Most Dictatorships in the World

What Is the Common Factor Between CNN and Mubarak?

Hail to the Chief: The Making and Unmaking of Moroccan Kings

Iran is a Model of Feminism for America:
When Descendants of Eve Run for President

Union of Words: A History of Castro's Eloquence

Death Squads in Jordanian *Moukhabarat* Are Legitimate:
Security Justifies Constraining Civil Liberties…and Also Lives

They Both Rule until Death, Are Not Voted into Office,
and Control their Herd

Very Low Juvenile Crimes in Tunisia: Efficiency in the Police Public System

Democracy's Big Day: The Bey'aa of the Moroccan king

You Steal My Wallet but I Can Still Be Your Friend:
Why Doesn't America Follow the Path of Oslo in Its War Against Terror?

More Students in Riots Back Home:
Empirical Proof That Avenues of Dissent Are Open for Third World Students

How Area studies experts see you

Apologetic Tone

Subjective Writing

Coffee Can Never Taste Like Milk

State Propaganda

Excessive Nationalism

Overgeneralization

Correlation Is Not Causality: Again!

You Have Mathematical Proofs but Beliefs Spoken in English
Are Far Better Than Numbers in Chinese

Where is the Exotic Morocco That We Want?

The typical reaction of the learned reader after laughing at this table is to inquire about the connection between this caricature and the book written by Hammoudi. Given that the book was written from *within the discipline* of anthropology and in the corridors of modern academia, it has to bear the imprint of what David Price, who teaches anthropology at St.Martin's College and who is researching the impact of McCarthyism on American anthropology, wrote a fascinating (or more sincerely fascinating me!) article that discusses a letter published by Franz Boaz and published in *The Nation*. In this article, morality is fortunately on the menu with the idea that *"a scientist who uses his research as a cover for political spying forfeits the right to be classified as a scientist."*[8] Among the points mentioned in this article, we can cite the facts that the American Anthropological Association (AAA) has no explicit clauses in its code of ethics concerning espionage, which made it easy for the Harvard archeologist Samuel Lothrop to spy for Naval Intelligence in the Caribbean during World War I. Moreover, the famous Norwegian sociologist Johan Galtung revealed that many anthropologists were working on counterinsurgency programs in Latin America under a project named Camelot. He goes back to the 1950s, when *"the AAA's executive board negotiated a secret agreement with the CIA under which agency personnel and computers were used to produce a cross-listed directory of AAA members, showing their geographical and linguistic areas of expertise along with summaries of research interests."*[9]

I am by no means saying here that Hammoudi is a spy, for I would be contradicting my Sufi teachings of pure intention as well as my academic scientism of skeptic stereotyping. My point here is that anthropology as a field would retain the contours of spying as a disciplining institution in a way that many anthropologists (without being aware of it) would find themselves replicating an "intelligent" discourse about the other by the mere fact of being obligated to follow the code of ethics and receive funds from CIA fronts like the Human Ecology Fund. Another instance where anthropology represents a threat for the analysis of Hammoudi is the critique that it receives from people like Akbar Ahmed and Edward Said—namely that it would create an essentialist view of what the Sufi is without inviting those who are in the path to participate in the theoretical construction of their identity. The existence of qualitative techniques such as interviewing does not solve the problem, because the "savage" is introduced only as a word in a text loaded with its own truths. Hammoudi gives voice in his account to some Sufi saints, but he still subjects their voice to a Foucauldian approach that is ontologically constructed outside of the Sufi framework. Would Hammoudi use a Sufi ontology to interpret what his saints tell him? Throughout the book, the answer remains negative. We can see that anthropologists have retreated to the politics of textuality, where the observer is not seriously addressed. Moreover, the fact that anthropology was born in a colonialist and orientalist environment where the non-European was depicted as the savage and the primitive opens our eyes to the fact that Hammoudi's resentment toward an ancient mystical belief stems from a haunting anthropologism.

Talal Asad voiced a similar concern when he criticized the way the Sufi/Salafi divide gives way to other dichotomies like rural/urban, oral/scriptural, or folk/elite. Vincent Cornell gives a view of the local when he corrects some assumptions made about Moroccan Sufism by anthropologists not too keen on the local hagiographical anthology of sainthood. He showed us that *"contrary to the assumptions of Alfred Bel, Ernest Gellner, and Clifford Geertz, I suggested that Moroccan Sufism (like Sufism everywhere) has an urban ethos, even when it is found in the countryside."*[10]

Cornell spelled out here how Sufis were urban, a thesis that is different from the typical analysis of mystical brotherhoods as rural. Hammoudi describes the gift in his article on Dar al-Mulk as a visible exchange of objects that *"reaffirms the obligation of service and obedience, on the one hand, and the patronage and favor of the prince, on the other."* Here he is following the steps of Geertzian symbolic anthropology, which would be amazing if it did not lose its enthusiasm when it comes to Western gifts. In an interesting article titled "High Priests of the Unknown" Robert Lee Hotz wrote: *"the Nobel Prize can influence research priorities and confer a remarkable-sometimes undeserved-moral authority on its winners. Now some wonder if there's a risk in creating a secular sainthood."*[11] Hence, the mere inclusion of third worldly gifts in anthropology and first worldly gifts in law or journalism, despite the fact that we are in both cases dealing with sainthood, opens our eyes to the hegemonic bias of the symbolic account of gifts.

If Hammoudi's account belongs to the field of education rather than that of anthropology then one is led to see a rationalist modernist view of education based solely on two senses: hearing and seeing. It is true that saliva and semen are present in his description, but since they are seen as vehicles of domination, one can see easily how discrediting other senses comes only when sight and hearing are taken as references to judge teaching. In Western academia *"smell, taste and touch are rarely engaged by the school curriculum, for these senses are not generally considered to provide 'ways to wisdom', but rather, only channels for pleasure or displeasure."*[12] Taste is opposed to learning in the West since food is not allowed in the classroom but only during breaks as an alternative to studying. From this account, Hammoudi will definitely be led to condemn taste in mystical learning as a vehicle of power. In the same way touch would lead a professor in western academia to the territory of pedophilia and harassment, it leads Hammoudi to call his academic 911 manifested as a negative depiction of learning through touch as homoerotic interplay since he notes the homoerotic relationship among some Sufis and their disciples. Conversely, in the same way sipping a cup of tea in Zen Buddhism leads to a higher level of consciousness, the kissing of the master's hands leads to ecstatic states.

In this part, anthropology as a field was diagnosed with a bias against the non-Western voices, either through a historical association of early anthropologists with intelligence officers or through the constraints that departments of anthropology within academia put on scholars belonging to this field. For example, in the example of saliva as an exchange device between the master and the disciple, the mere depiction of this transaction as homoerotic cannot be done outside the boxes of a culture that is not familiar with same-sex touch in a platonic way. Any anthropological account deprived of the idea that *baraka* transcends homoeroticism depicts the idea of physical contact between the master and the disciple and therefore this saliva reminds us of the divine breath rather than an invitation to gather under the "gay rainbow." We have deconstructed so far the first brick of authoritarianism in Hammoudi's analysis by showing the anthropological foundations of his concept of power, so our first counterpoint is that anthropology as used by Hammoudi might push him to see authoritarianism in the mystical paradigm. If we use education as our paradigm because the nature of the relationship between the master and the disciple is an educational process, we will find out that traditional ways of teaching involve all the senses, and thus saliva is a container of knowledge rather than a lubricant of the anal region.

B) Taha Abderrahmane's Integrated Approach: An Alternative Explanation

Taha Abderrahmane is a Moroccan philosopher who mainly studies philosophy of language and Heidegger's concept of being. He started a project named *fiqh al falsafa* which we will translate as philopraxis. *Fiqh* is an Arabic word that joins knowledge and action, besides its usual meaning as jurisprudence. What characterizes Taha's work is the integrated approach that uses *internal* tools to assess a tradition. Whenever we are in front of a traditional text, the theory says, we should make sure that our methodology when analyzing this text is in line with the methodology of that tradition. If we are to interpret an Islamic text or event, we have to know that this text was written in Arabic as the language of the Koran[13] in accordance with an Islamic creed of unity (*Tawhid*) with an implicit reliance on assumptions from the Islamic information system. Language, faith, and information are to be present in the minds of those willing to engage in a genealogical work about Islamic culture. To use a language that is academically correct, I would say that this integrated approach takes as pillars, etymology, doxology, and epistemology whenever it deciphers signs of a tradition. Let us take the two first main ideas of Hammoudi's work and assess them according to our integrated approach. The first idea is building a parallel between the master-disciple relation and the king-subject symbiosis. In his preface, Hammoudi shows us the big picture of his work:

"*Building on Foucault's notion of diagramme, I describe how sets of emotional relations, such as Master/Disciple, evolved in mystic initiation, extended beyond Sufi circles, and attained a new credibility as the main operator of power relations,*"[14]

"*This book analyzes the transfer of mystic guidance in initiation to the realm of power relations and political institutions.*"[15]

"*My basic hypotheses in this book are as follows: inversion and ambivalence still constitute the cultural schema in terms of which access to any position of dominance is defined. Furthermore, this schema is grounded and sanctified by the* concepts and procedures involved in the process of mystical initiation."[16]

"This book was inspired by an issue that has haunted Arab intellectuals. It can be expressed in various ways, but the central question is constant: how can we account for the prevalence of authoritarian political systems in our societies, from the Atlantic to the Gulf?"[17]

It is interesting to notice that Hammoudi does not want us to read his book as "a solipstic exercise in political lucidity nor as a rejection of the mystic path toward spiritual self-fulfillment and salvation in communal or individual forms."[18] By quoting him we want to spare the reader the unfounded doubt that we are constructing a straw-man fallacy by refuting Hammoudi's rejection of Sufism. We are not saying that he is rejecting Sufism in his book, but we are checking the assertion that the mystical path is a cultural root of political authoritarianism in Morocco. As a hors-d'oeuvre, it is interesting to listen to diZerega, who has an alternative view when he says that Eastern societies "have little to teach the West about politics. Fruitful instruction will be the other way around. But the undemocratic character of Eastern *civilizations is not itself a reflection on Eastern spiritual insights."*[19] John Voll presents the counterpoint to Hammoudi's foundation of authoritarianism when he writes:

> *"The authoritarianism that has failed is not the authoritarianism of traditional society. The authoritarianism that has failed is that of the regimes which are the products of the modernization of North African States that followed major Western models. It is, therefore, Western authoritarianism that is in crisis in North Africa.*[20]

Authoritarianism stems then from the use of a bureaucratic model foreign to the social landscape, creating practices like corruption and nepotism. But since the traditional system does not die at all, it serves the purpose of justifying those practices according to a religious commandment. Corruption is justified as gift and nepotism is viewed as solidarity. The main point to learn from John Voll is that Western authoritarianism is responsible for the delay in development, not tradition.

1) Moroccan Sainthood Does Not Speak Latin

According to the integrated approach, the language of a "studied" tradition is part of its ontology. Hence, when analyzing the link between master and disciple, Hammoudi has to account for the Arabic concepts used in the tradition that he is exploring. He engages indeed in this etymological fundamentalism (in the sense of coming back to the fundamentals) only with the concept of *shaykh*, one of the Arabic names for master. He tells us how *"a mystical master attributes to himself the title of shaykh-which designates anyone who claims some preeminence, whether he be a master in exoteric and esoteric sciences, master artisan, tribal chief, neighborhood chief, father-in-law (for a married woman), older person, or older."*[21] I am allergic to two sins committed by the author here. First, it is a sin of omission when the author comes back to the etymology of the Arabic name for master (*Shaykh*) but "forgets" to take the same road with the other half of the relation, namely the disciple (*Murid*). Second, it is a sin when he says that the mystical master *"attributes to himself the title of shaykh"* or when he equates this title with anybody *"who claims some preeminence."*

With respect to the second sin, the *shaykh* in a Sufi brotherhood does not claim his title; nor does he attribute it to himself. In order to become a spiritual master, it is required to have two legitimating stamps: one from a paranormal world through dreams (and of course this road cannot be "analyzed" by non-mystical sciences) and the other from a living master who explicitly designs his or her successor before death comes. The rationalistic mind accepts without problems the second legitimacy "model" but finds a hard time separating the first "model" from authoritarianism. In fact, when a disciple receives this divine message it is not left to a chaotic interpretation but is regulated by two conditions: generally the message comes as a dream or a vision in which the prophet Mohammed (peace be upon him) brings the potential master the tidings of his responsibility, and this dream or vision is subjected to the hermeneutical explanation of an authority who interprets dreams and in most cases it is the living master. If one knows enough the prophetic tradition, the first thing that comes to mind is the *hadith,* in which the prophet himself says that whoever sees him in a dream is *really seeing him* because Satan cannot take the prophetic form. Once the authenticity of the *hadith* is established it is impossible for a *believer* (the one who leaves his skeptical shoes at the gate of the Islamic information system) to reject such an avenue. Furthermore, the "inaugural dream" is seen not only by the master-to-be but also by his master and numerous other people on the path. Even the law of coincidence stops in front of the hill of repetition. Hence, when more than one person sees it, and especially when their interests and backgrounds do not waltz together, we are close to the territory of participation. Thus, once this investiture is approved by an authority agreed upon by a former authority, is beyond any suspicion from the members of the community, and confirmed is not only by the members of this community but also by superior forces whose authority is infinite (God and angels), it is acceptable to shout "Democracy!"

Sufis believe in the existence of a paranormal council of saints in charge of the matters of this world, where decisions are made by the consensus of those wise people. If one accepts that in a civilization that depends exclusively on the worldly matters (the American political system), it is the electoral college and not the voice of the masses that determines the leader of the nation. Why should we reject the notion of an "unseen electoral college" for a civilization where the seen and the unseen cohabit peacefully? One counterargument here is, how can we prevent a dictator from claiming that he has the democratic support of a ghostly council? My argument goes as follows. There are two types of leaderships; one is exoteric and the second is esoteric. The former comes to power with tools belonging to the nature of its outward tasks. Presidents, kings, and sultans fall into this category and instead of relying on an invisible endorsement of a high intelligence, they derive their legitimacy from voting or allegiance (*beyaa*). The latter refers to Sufis and saints, who do not come to power in an arbitrary fashion but use a methodology from the sanctum of their paradigm and in line with their hidden task. Hence, they rely on a legitimacy derived from a collectivity belonging to another dimension, because the task that is assigned to them is indeed of an esoteric nature. "Angelocracy" for beginners would ask the following questions: Why aren't intelligence experts in America "voted" into office? How come their actions are not exposed to the public gaze? The answer is the risk of jeopardizing national security. It is because the work of intelligence agencies is mostly undercover that it is nonsensical to publicize what is beneath its veil. Even the courageous Freedom of Information Act under which masses *could* have access to classified documents is constrained by national security. When it comes to the presidency, an institution equated more and more with political entertainment, Jay Leno and his fellows can use their imaginations to make jokes about a public figure. But even then, because of his busy agenda, a president cannot be sued for civil infractions. We are here at the core of political and legal orientalism when dictatorship becomes legitimate only by wearing the outfit of law.

I will not ask if Hammoudi's sin of not tracing the Arabic etymology of the other half of the pair that he studied (the disciple) is a deliberate or a subliminal action, but I will look for the authentic word of the disciple in the Sufi tradition. The Arabic word for disciple is *Murid*, and it comes from the verb *arada*, which means to will or to want. *Irada* is the action of this verb and can be translated as will. Furthermore, the word *Murid* comes in a semantic structure reserved in Arabic to active subjects and called *Ism fa'il* meaning literally "name of the doer." The semantic questioning of the term *disciple* leads us to conclude that one submits *willingly and actively* to the master. One can of course object here and bring counterarguments used by Gramsci and Camus as to the fact that submitting with will to hegemony does not turn it into a "good" act. I agree wholly with that but unfortunately this is a straw-man fallacy here because it misses my main argument. Hammoudi singled out Morocco and the Arab world with his model of master and disciple, and it is against this singularity that I posit my thesis of a hegemonic contract. Now, if one shifts the level of analysis to Camus and Gramsci when power and hegemony become invisible, my point is that the singularity of the Moroccan case vanishes, since even in the most evolved democracy's lamb tends to be the most popular animal willingly voting its butchers into office.

What about a little comparative philology stretching? The word *disciple* is a Middle English name coming from the Latin verb *discere*, which means "to learn." The Merriam-Webster's dictionary has two definitions for a disciple: *"a convinced adherent of a school or individual"* and *"a member of the Disciples of Christ founded in the U.S. in 1809 that holds the Bible alone to be the rule of faith and practice, usually baptizes by immersion, and has a congregational polity."* The six definitions given by the same dictionary to the term *discipline* are very interesting: *"Punishment, obsolete: Instruction, a field of study, training that corrects, molds, or perfects the mental faculties or moral character, control gained by enforcing obedience or order and a rule or system of rules governing conduct or activity."* It is very normal for Hammoudi to be drawn to the coercive and punitive definitions of discipline when he fed from the breast of Foucault, whose work *Discipline and Punish* is a genealogical description of the birth and evolution of *punishment.*

2) Mysticism and the Creed of Unity

Before studying any mystical brotherhood in order to analyze the ambivalences and inversions in the relationship between master and disciple, one has to notice the prevalence of an exogenous approach in studying mysticism in the Islamic culture. It is common to see among political scientists, sociologists, and anthropologists a tendency to "study" any Islamic movement as a social movement with categorizations such as radical/moderate, Sunni/Sufi, or modern/traditional. Hence, generalizations are engineered wherein Islamic revivals are correlated with a shortage of food and wherein religious differences between Islamic groups are ignored or looked at from a sociological perspective. It is hence no surprise to find scholars in religious sciences, such as Sachiko Murata and John Esposito, who are successful in understanding Islamic social movements because they start from *the revelatory texts of those movements* in order to understand the rationale of their behavior and assess the reality of their "threat."

Rather than treating Islamic movements as one subset of *rogue movements*, it is worth knowing the classification criteria that should be used when putting these movements "in drawers." I have always found Eastern religious scholars more *able* and more *willing* to understand, communicate, and exchange with the Muslims both at the scholastic and the "mundane" aspects of life. Their *ability* stems from the fact that their cultural revolution made them immune to the destructive sides of Enlightenment rationality, and their *willingness* comes from the fact that they are not associated with a North too blinded by a technological superiority to listen to the message of those poor people that Fanon called *The Wretched of the Earth* of the world. It is no wonder to find that Sachiko Murata and William Chittick use a prophetic tradition to separate Allah's last revelation into *Islam* (submission), *Iman* (faith), and *Ihsan* (doing what is beautiful). The text of the *Hadith* of Gabriel goes as follows:

> *"Umar ibn al-khattab said: One day when we were with God's messenger, a man with very white clothing and very black hair came up to us. No mark of travel was visible on him, and none of us recognized him. Sitting down before*

the Prophet, leaning his knees against his, and placing his hands on his thighs, he said, 'Tell me, Muhammad, about submission.'

He replied, 'Submission means that you should bear witness that there is no god and that Muhammad is God's messenger, that you should perform the ritual prayer, pay the alms tax, fast during Ramadan, and make the pilgrimage to the house if you are able to go there.'

The man said, 'you have spoken the truth.' We were surprised at his questioning him and then declaring that he had spoken the truth. He said: 'Now tell me about your faith.' He replied: 'Faith means that you have faith in God, His angels, his books, his messengers, and the Last Day, and that you have faith in the measuring out, both its good and its evil.' Remarking that he had spoken the truth he then said: 'Now tell me about doing what is beautiful.'

He replied: 'Doing what is beautiful means that you should worship God as if you see him, for even if you do not see him, he sees you'…"[22]

According to Murata and Chittick *"the hadith of Gabriel suggests that in Islamic understanding, religion embraces right ways of doing things, right ways of thinking and understanding, and right ways of forming the intentions that lie behind the activity."*[23] In other words, an integral approach in and of Islam would see events in terms of their context, content, and intent. The two last dimensions are somehow missing in Hammoudi's analysis of the link between the mystical and the political arenas. When he found a similarity between the brotherhood and the political party based on the idea of appointments rather than elections, or historical rather than democratic legitimacy, he was only looking at the *external structure* of both paths. Positively speaking, from his brilliant remark that brotherhoods look like parties, he went on to fall into the "Statistics 101" fallacy of correlation as causality. He notices that *"if the royal institution and its legitimacy function in and through the hegemony of sainthood, as has been noted, it seems logical to consider the master-disciple relationship in Sufi initiation as the decisive schema for the construction of Power relations."*[24] He does not hide his desire to see *"legal rationality"* sweep away the primitive irrational dust in political relationships when he reveals how *"the master-disciple example not only continues to inform political interaction in present-*

day Morocco but still appears hegemonic in comparison with other modes. Far from being driven away by a new legal rationality, the master's authority pervades bureaucracy." [25]

I am pretty much uncomfortable with the idea of raising "legal rationality" to the station of a "safety valve" or an ultimate stage of democracy to be worshipped in Morocco not only because I can hardly walk in the footsteps of those who purport an end of history with the advent of free market ideology and liberal democracy, but also because I see liberal democracy as having the same "authoritarianism" criticized by Hammoudi. The idea of diplomatic immunity or presidential vetoes and pardons fall into this category that will be analyzed carefully later. Here, once the diagnosis is made that the master-disciple framework is the seed of political authoritarianism, Hammoudi decides to replace it by legal rationality. In other words, he finds problematic the way that religion is politicized and presents a secular solution separating *zawiya* and *state*. I join Hammoudi in condemning the politicization of ethics, but instead of opting for an easy divorce, I prefer to see an "ethicization" of politics.

The idea of *Iman* from the earlier *Hadith* is very relevant here. It is not because a political party is caught erring while *dressed in the coat* of the mystics that Sufism should be blamed for this authoritarian tendency. When *intent* is introduced as a variable, one sees why this mystical structure fails when "shipped" to the partisan sea. The master-disciple framework has God as its goal, and thus any submission to the master comes with the *intention* of serving God, because according to mystics, masters are emissaries of God who embody the Mohammedan light. In a prophetic *hadith*, the prophet Muhamad says that *"the most frightening thing that I fear for my community is associating others with God. I do not mean to say that they will worship the sun, or the moon or idols. I mean that they will perform works for other than God with a hidden desire."* [26] A party in Arab societies is generally serving a nationalistic, an ethnical, or an ideological goal where the intention to serve God hardly appears. Therefore, replicating the exoteric mystical aspect without its internal legacy (unity in intention) would definitely produce a power politics paradigm with mystical appearance, and we surely remember that not everything that shines is gold.

When *context* is introduced, one notices that one essential variable is missing in the political party structure: divine authorization or *idhn*. Mystics believe that unless an action is authorized by the divine, it is seedless even if it appears to be shining. In other words, when we want to explore power in mystical and partisan paths, we should look inside the Islamic tradition to see whether this obedience has certain legitimacy. When God created Adam from clay and drew his spirit into the clay shape, he asked all the angels to prostrate in front of this clay creation. Only Satan or *Iblis* refused to obey the command because he said that since he was created from fire, he was not to prostrate in front of an "inferior" creation. Satan stayed at the level of the *eye* (which interestingly enough matches the '*I*' at a phonological level) in the sense that he only saw the external aspect of Adam. The angels obeyed the Lord because they respected the divine breath in Adam's shape and hence went beyond the exoteric cover.

Let us pick one story narrated in the *Hadith* literature and then derive some lessons from it using a Sufi methodology of unity and commonality.

> *"The story goes that one day Muhammad's foster-brothers had rushed to their parents, crying in terror that two men in white had seized Muhammad and had seemed to slit his belly open. Halima had rushed to the scene to find the little boy lying weakly on the ground: later he explained that the men had*

taken his heart from his body and washed it with snow; then

they had lifted him on to a pair of scales and declared that he

was heavier than all the rest of the Arabs put together." [27]

The event in question refers to the incident of "heart surgery" performed by the angel Gabriel on a child who was going to become a messenger (Muhammad). Karen Armstrong understands well the symbolic meaning of such a message when she sees the story as being *"similar to legends in other cultures describing an initiation: it symbolizes the purity that is necessary if the initiate is to receive an experience of the divine without tainting the sacred message."* [28] We will learn from this historical fact the following lessons:

- Any human being born with a defect in the heart needs a "surgical operation" to clean the polluted organ.

- The surgical operation is not performed by the holder of the organ but rather by an angelic being coming from the divine realm.

- Reason is not to be separated from emotion since the locus of the operation was not the head but the heart. That is why in Syrian dialect we find the expression *"balek fi kalbek"* (let your mind be in your heart).

The second legitimating tool from the Islamic creed is the idea of the primeval covenant between God and Adam as a spokesperson of the human species. This covenant is described in the following verse of the Koran: "*When your Lord drew forth from the Children of Adam, from their loin, their descendants and made them testify concerning themselves [saying] "Am I not your Lord?" they said, "Yes, we do testify" [this], lest you should say on the Day of Judgment: "of this we were unaware" (7:172)*. This covenant between God and *all* his creation is very significant since it reunites reason and revelation as well as universalism and particularity. Both reason and revelation are God-made. (Is not the intellect a gift from God?). And the discernment of divine laws comes through the remembrance of the covenant. [29]

In the covenant, God made a contract (Divine contracts are not betrayed unlike human ones.) with Adam and all the human species that their reason will be "right" as long as it is *bounded* by his remembrance. Adam signed the contract. *Reason* in Arabic is *aql*, a name coming from *aqala*, meaning to attach or to bind (hence the concept of bounded rationality). Revelation is said to be a divine reason according to the Adamic covenant. Moreover, *aql* never came as a noun in the Koran but rather as a verb taking its seat in the heart. Reason is *a human revelation* and revelation is *a divine reason*. Revelation can be described as *a natural reason* and reason is seen as an *artificial revelation*. Finally, reason can be called an *internal revelation*. Meanwhile, revelation would be an *external reason*. Reason and revelation are flipsides of the same coin in the divine realm, which leaves us no room for an antagonism between *dhikr* (remembrance) and *fikr* (reason).

These legitimating texts are not reported at all by Hammoudi in his account of the issue of obedience, an oblivion that leads him to draw unfounded parallels and knock out fictional targets. He says in his book that *"all prayers would be in vain without the assistance of a living master (al shaykh al hay). Seeking his help in a totally submissive manner overrides all other conditions and constitutes the sine qua non for success. So it seems that success, manifested by access to masterhood (which is the goal of every initiation), is first and foremost dependent on continuous closeness to Shaykh, as well as faultless allegiance to his commands and his person."*[30] It is completely erroneous—yet *realpolitikally* correct— to think that the goal of the disciple is to become a master. I happen to be a disciple and becoming a master has never crossed my heart (at least not before I read Hammoudi), and one can tell here the positivist influence behind this idea of obeying power only to seek it and appropriate it. In fact, a Moroccan proverb says that the best of humans are those who are more willing to serve the people (*sid rjal khdimhoum*). It is equally erroneous to think that the love of a disciple toward the master is similar to that felt by the subject toward the king, since the former is a pure love (*hubb atta'alluk*) and the latter a pragmatic one (*hubb attamalluk*). Furthermore, the gift that a subject gives to a leader has to be of a high value in order not to generate the wrath of his majesty, and it is very close to the territory of corruption, unlike the gift presented to the spiritual master called *ziara*, meaning visit. The *ziara* can be of any value and is there just as a purifying tool according to the verse of the Koran wherein God asks his prophet to take from the Muslims' money a portion of charity to *raise* and *purify* them (*tuzakkihim wa tutahhiruhum biha*).

Finally, obedience on a spiritual path follows a voluntary allegiance to the master (*bey'aa*) where the disciple makes a social contract (in line with the primeval covenant) in which he shows his *trust* of the master in this remembrance journey. If the Sufi obedience is based on *trust*, the realist obedience is based on *dissent*. The positivist mind subjects the performance of leadership to the checks and balances of reason. This idea assumes that reason will be able in all instances (even for national security there is freedom of information) to comprehend the business of the bosses. The Sufi framework is modeled after the story between Moses and one of God's emissaries in the chapter *al kahf* in the Koran, wherein Moses asks the servant to whom he was sent by God sent him: *"May I follow thee, on the footing that thou teach me something of the Truth which Thou hast been taught?"* The servant replied: *"Verily, Thou will not be able to bear patience with me,"* telling him that he will encounter things that his reason cannot admit, and asked him not to ask him any questions about what will come until he himself makes mention of it. Moses accepted the deal and said: *"Thou will find me, if Allah so will, patient nor shall I disobey you in aught."* The story continues and Moses asks him three times when the latter saw that he killed an innocent child, damaged the boat of innocent people, and helped those who refused to provide shelter for those building a falling wall. The humble servant says then: *"This is the parting between thee and me: now I will show thee the interpretation of that with which thou could not have patience."* Regarding the boat, he told him that it belonged to those who were in dire need of it and that there was a king who seized every boat by force so he could render it mildly unserviceable. Moses could not accept the idea of digging a hole in a boat because for him water meant danger and drowning, yet had he recalled his youth, he would have found that as a baby his mother had had to put him in water to survive. Often we miss our own developmental history and we think that injustices that face us are victimizing us. In fact, a good blessing from a sincere mother can travel and reach a great grandson in the genealogy of time, and no wonder then that the Native Americans advised us to always act with the well-being of the seventh generation in mind.

3) Islamic Information System 101

The first obstacle that occurs to our mind is the way of presenting a whole legacy in few pages without forgetting its essential foundations or simplifying what is complex. It should be noted though that *saying the same thing to everybody at the same time and in the same place* is a product of Enlightenment education. In Sufism an expression has many meanings and many audiences. As a listener a disciple should interpret what his or her master says, bearing in mind the following principles:

- Knowledge has also a time for which audiences should be ripe. Knowledge is not information.

- A master does not aim only at informing when speaking. His or her words reflect a state of being that the disciple is supposed to reach. If the disciple is already in that state, the master's saying might be a correction of the disciple's flaws. If the disciple is not yet in that state of being, he or she should strive to reach it. Ellipsis is a mode of expression in the land of the Sufis and *it is meant to remain their mother tongue.* Expression/ellipsis is a fake dichotomy that many scholars and even many Muslims quote to mention the uniqueness of the Sufi language. There is no mutual exclusion between expression and ellipsis. Let us use a time-space framework to account for the symbiosis between these two figures of speech. An ellipsis is an expression *in prospect.* An expression is an ellipsis *in retrospect.* An ellipsis will become an expression when its significance is unveiled by the disciple, so every ellipsis is to be deciphered in the future. In terms of space, every ellipsis is an *internal* expression and every expression is an *external* ellipsis. What constitutes an ellipsis for me might be an expression for others or, to use an analogy coined by Geertz, the same gesture might be perceived as a wink or as a blink. In the Sufi paradigm, realities are multiple and holistic where statements are idiographic rather than nomothetic. In simple English, it means that Sufi hypotheses are context-bound rather than context-free. When it comes to causality, all entities are in mutual reshaping in a way that one cannot set a temporal precedence for causality. If we are to set an analogy, we can safely call Sufism a *quantum religion* in the sense that mystical principles (like those of Taoism) better fit the Western model of quantum physics rather than Cartesian or Newtonian reality. In this manner Hammoudi needs cosmetic surgery so that he can join the wave of quantum anthropology. We will try to define the Islamic Information System in this part in a way that the pitfalls of Hammoudi become our guide to the exploration of the Sufi principles. Starting from the critique of Geertz, whose influence on Hammoudi is clear, we will trace those pitfalls back to their dogmatic roots to provide an alternative explanation from within the Sufi paradigm.

There are basically three problems with the analysis of Clifford Geertz in *Islam Observed*. First, he forced imported interpretation with Freudian overtones on local symbols. In fact, Henry Munson shows us in his marvelous book *Religion and Power in Morocco* how the process of reconstructing the collective imagination of seventeenth-century Morocco *"without recourse to the texts in which it is inscribed is like trying to interpret a poem in a language one does not read."* [31] Second, he reduced *Baraka* (a concept loosely translated as charisma) to personality traits unable to reflect Moroccan specificity. With a touch of sarcasm, Munson shows a certain academic incorrectness toward those general personality traits when he writes that *"extraordinary physical courage, absolute personal loyalty, and ecstatic moral intensity can be found among Kamikaze pilots, revolutionaries, and religious zealots all over the world."* [32] Belief is narrowed down to personality in Geertz's Islam and *"because of his neglect of the religious framework in which the notion of Baraka is rooted, Geertz is unable to understand this social fact and its political implications."* [33] In light of this view, the cultural space becomes only an identity marker. Third, he sets up a dichotomy between miraculous and genealogical *Baraka* in the story between a Moroccan King of the Alawi Dynasty in the Seventeenth Century and al-Yusi, a saint and a religious scholar who used to be his advisor to become a dissident later. Geertz reached the conclusion that in the Alawi Dynasty there was supremacy of genealogical over miraculous *Baraka*. Geertz sees indeed this conflict between a saint and a sultan *"as representing a conflict between traditional, miraculous form of saintly baraka, and its newer, genealogical form, represented by the Sharifian Alawi dynasty."*[34]

Munson does not agree with this dichotomy because, according to the local people that he interviewed—and he was certainly vaccinated in his doctoral field research courses against sampling bias—al-Yusi had both aspects of *baraka*, a fact that would make it absurd to fight for something already acquired. If the local barefooted indigenous academic guinea pigs who offer shelter, food, and a great sense of hospitality to researchers willing to "make interesting contributions to the field" decreed that a separation between the miraculous and the genealogical is a pathological misperception, let us leave the floor for a Moroccan Eighteenth Century historian named al-Qadiri to interpret this clash between the crown and the turban. The indigenous historian *"informs us that Mulay Ismail feared al-Yusi because he attracted many followers and could have lead or encouraged the periodic Berber revolts that the sultan spent years trying to suppress."* [35] A new variable makes its appearance with the advent of Moroccan historiography: ethnicity. Rather than—or probably in parallel to—interpreting the *Moroccan crown-fight* (a rhythmic equivalent of *Balinese Cockfight*) as a clash of saints and sultans, one can see it as belligerency between Arabs and Berbers.

It should be obvious that this critical taxonomy of the tools used by Geertz to observe Islam is by no means a campaign against an anthropological dinosaur, but rather a forensic exploration of Geertzian DNA in the body of Hammoudi. As a matter of fact, the author of *Master and Disciple* does not interpret mystical practices wearing lenses belonging to that "field." The main logical tag that Hammoudi is wearing in this anthropological journey is *causality*. If we were to put his whole book in a positivist logical form (a practice baptized by our fellows from the quantitative planet operationalization) we would say mysticism causes authoritarianism when dressed in a political suit. To give weight to my unripe analysis, I would call on Peter Winch to express his disagreement with the colonial anthropological study of Zande magic by MacIntyre and Evans-Pritchard. Winch denies the existence of a monolithic concept of causal influence in the West in the following remark:

"When we speak, for example, of 'what made Jones get married', we are not saying the same kind of thing as when we speak of 'what made the aero-plane crash'; I do not mean simply that the events of which we speak are different in kind but that the relation between the events is different also. It should not then be difficult to accept that in a society with quite different institutions and ways of life from our own, there may be concepts of 'causal influence' which behave even more differently." [36]

Winch comes back to the Judeo-Christian prayer of supplication in the story of Job (the expression "if it be thy will") to tell us that whenever we see this prayer as *a way of influencing an outcome*, we will ignore the believer's perspective of the prayer as an *emancipation from the dependence on the subject of supplication.* If one inhabits a glass house, throwing stones is not the *smartest* action to undertake. Similarly, if one is drowning in an ocean of causality and power, prospects of emancipation are not the *brightest* thing to see. Hammoudi, by failing to use his own cultural legacy, falls into the materialist trap of seeing mysticism as a bad way of producing consumer goods (power) since authoritarianism is a public "bad" (in lieu of a public good). A Sufi looks at the mystical abode as a mode of life-regulating vertical (divine) and horizontal (social) relations and not only as a vagina or a penis *producing* power. Hammoudi seems to see the master-disciple relationship in terms of *"efficiency of production"* in the same way that an "almighty bucks" person sees a friend as a walking portfolio and in the same fashion that a superpower sees its orbiting peripheries as disposable condoms worn while penetrating other strategic sanctuaries.

The new paradigms in political theory, carrying the seeds of the quantum revolution in physics, question the separation between subject and object, and the focus on *persons* rather than *relationships*. A subject involved in the study of a project affects the outcome of the studied object. Moreover, there are no boundaries in quantum physics and system theory. This Western scientific mode of thinking is similar to the very old Eastern traditions, as is shown by Fritjof Capra in his *Tao of Physics*. Tu Wei-Ming puts this idea into the following wise statement:

> *"To Confucians, Taoists, and Buddhists, knowledge is enlightenment, a power of self-illumination. And only in its corrupt form does knowledge become a power of conquest. According to*

this line of thinking, to be fully human requires the courage and wisdom of constantly harmonizing oneself with an ever-enlarging network of relationships, which necessitates a perspective going beyond the restrictions of anthropocentrism." [37]

The priority of relationships over objects is a phenomenon that is "proved" empirically by cybernetics, dissipative structures in chemistry, neurology, and transpersonal psychology. Only political science is still using a Newtonian clock essentially because it harbors some people who failed in their "pure science" fields and ended up gaining some fame in "social science," most often because most of their audience does not understand their statistical mumbling. When *Baraka* is defined only as a personality charisma, it automatically leads to a negative connotation because the "stick" can only be within the hands of the person holding the *Baraka*. Since we are here in a symbiotic relationship, portraying the source of power (*Baraka*) as an asset held only by one side of the relationship fails to meet the Eastern and the postmodern views of privileging relations over objects or persons. In fact, when we see charisma seated in a person rather than in a *relationship*, we will definitely be drawn to magnify the side where this charisma lies. The *master* will definitely be seen as a *monster* in this narrative. Di Zerega notices that *"within the atomistic framework, coercion is generally defined as the unauthorized crossing of boundaries, either of a person or of property. But we cannot find an objective criterion for boundaries. By contrast, the relational framework rejects coercion because it is a bad way for two or more people to relate."* [38]

Hammoudi falls in the trap of dealing with the question of sainthood in an anthropomorphic form where knowledge is treated as a commodity and a source of authoritative power. This way of seeing things is definitely not Moroccan, so Hammoudi must have brought it from somewhere. We can see again how Hammoudi rarely uses texts from within the Sufi paradigm to assess a reality loaded with symbols. Hammoudi is highly influenced by the theory of personality that stresses personal traits without leaving much room for social networks. Glen Oaks,[39] a scholar of religion, has developed an explanation of charisma on the basis of the theory of personality. Starting from the idea that Jesus represents the archetype of prophetic charisma in the West, Oaks makes *narcissism* one of the pillars of the charismatic personality. A narcissistic person is known for its self-proclaimed *grandeur* and a desire to control others as a defense mechanism against a haunting feeling of weakness. In Oakes's analysis, the narcissistic personality produces two types of prophets: the *messianic* and the *charismatic*. Many charismatic leaders share characteristics of both types. The messianic prophet strives for a truth outside him- or herself. On the contrary, the charismatic prophet is absorbed by an ideal from within. The lives of both prophetic types are characterized by five psychological stages: *early narcissism* during childhood, *incubation* in the sense of a prophetic calling (*Da'wah*), *awakening* manifest in the adoption of a prophetic role, and *mission* of founding an organization to spread the word and *decline* in leadership. Oaks wrote his book as an alternative to Weber's definition of charisma as a social relationship where the community validates the "claim" of those invested with divine authority. Hammoudi overlooks Weber's model by reducing charisma to its personality traits and seems to touch upon it only when he sits a dichotomy between the sultan and the saint, which is a nice mask for Geertz's miraculous and genealogical forms of *Baraka*. In fact, the genealogical charisma is about a linear historical privilege of belonging to an "other" (the prophet) that confers the charismatic legitimacy. This dichotomy is similar to the one drawn by Oaks between a messianic and a charismatic prophet. However, Hammoudi never succeeds in blurring the line dividing the two types. Had Hammoudi searched in the authentic Islamic *Hadith* literature, he would have found that this separation is a pure fantasy engineered by Geertz's "interpretation of culture" rather than some genuine desire to bring 'truth' from the "local knowledge." The prophet Muhammad (PBUH) has left us two narrations regarding this issue of genealogical charisma. The first one clearly states that he left us two safety valves against deviance from the right path: the holy book and his members of family (*ahl-albait*). On the other hand, he left a narration-advice to his own members of family, warning them about coming with nothing but their lineage on the judgment day, when others will be judged according to their deeds. If we were to engage in a rhythmic play of words, we would say that *deeds* and *seeds* tango together in the land of the Sufis.

How do Sufis regard the relationship between the master and the disciple? In all esoteric teachings, the disciple in relation to her master is called the "child of the spirit." The Arabic expression is *tifl al-maani*, which is written (when using the Latin alphabet) in the same way we would write the "child of semen," since *maani* in Arabic means also semen. When using an Arab transliteration, the difference between the two words is accounted for. *Maani* means semen, while *M'aani* means spirit and is the parallel of matter or *mabani*. Hence, from our morphological surgery we can notice that spirit and semen are not separated in the case where Arab transliteration is absent. What the transliteration does is introduce the phonetic " ' " as a way of writing the Arabic sound *'ain* that also means eye—a word that in turn rhymes phonetically with the pronoun 'I'. At the end of this linguistic chain we find that it is the eye and the 'I' that determine whether spirit and semen mean the same thing. When one forgets Arabic phonetics, the child of the spirit equals the child of semen.[40] This is the road taken by Hammoudi when he regards the transmission of saintly *baraka* to the disciple as *insemination*. In fact, he affirms that the disciple is "*impregnated through a teaching process which resembles procreation.*"[41] This point can only indicate that this assimilation of the flow of energetic forces from the saint to the disciple with the ejaculation of semen is viable only when the linguistic specificity of Arabic is *ignored*. One can say here that this argument from within is a mere phonological delusion lacking the rigor of scientific verifiability. However, turning a blind eye to a common practice in all esoteric paths (*letters as embodying meaning*) is simply adopting a *literalist-fundamentalist* approach that is not very welcome among postmodern scholars.

In the Hebrew tradition, the first stage in the meditation ladder according to the Kabala is *emanation*, which is called *Ein*, meaning "nothing," as a reflection that the being in development develops out of nothing. Not only do we see here an acoustical resemblance between *Ein* and the Arabic sound *'Ain*, but we also see that if emanation comes from nothing we cannot speak about procreation. In Hinduism, the child of the spirit is called the golden germ (*hiranya-garbha*). This relationship transcends even Eastern traditions since "*just as Nietzsche was able to conceive of the Superman, Stanley Kubrick and Arthur Clarke were able to conceive the Star-Child in their science-fiction movie/novel 2001: A Space Odyssey.*"[42] Is the recourse to a semantic analysis of semen relevant here? Hammoudi speaks about semen when he uses his framework of *inversion* in his analysis of the relationship between a master and his or her disciples, and we are saying that it is not Moroccan or local knowledge, given our previous philological stretching (and of course the critique about this stretching as rising neither to the *power* nor to the *magnitude* of shaking anthropological idols is totally acceptable).

C) Foucault and A Gender-Friendly Master and Disciple

One of the main flaws in this beautiful narrative about Sufi orders is its *a-historical* nature, and its *"patriarchal definition"* of gender. Brooke Olson clearly finds the same faults with the book analyzed here in the sense that starting from an individual case of Sufism to infer generalizations about the whole mystical paradigm is a logical error that, if put in other contexts, would generate scholarly comments like "beware of reductionism." The book reviewer saw with finesse that *"given the many Sufi groups still active in Morocco, as well as a plethora of documentary sources available for various historical groups, it seems odd that Hammoudi relies only on one nineteenth-century biography of the Sufi master Sidi al-Haj 'Ali to create this model."*[43] Had Hammoudi been more familiar with the Sufi framework, he would have known that being the "son of the moment" (*ibn al waqt*) is one of the main Sufi expressions. Therefore, the tools used in the Sufi initiation are context-bound and are either changed or eliminated. Relying on "old" hagiographic analyses to account for a Sufi reality in our age is not rendering service to the historical requirements of the political culture school to which the author belongs. Hammoudi was indeed aware of this situation when he wrote an article after the publication of his book. He found himself "*reduced to a reconstruction beginning in the present, running the risk of abusing the past by projecting onto it contemporary categories of analysis.*" [44]

Why does the author fail in this reductionism? In page 85 of his book, he assumes that the master-disciple relationship has "*achieved a high degree of homogeneity,*" justifying the generalization to other mystical relations. In his article written in 1999, Hammoudi was aware of the weakness of his justification, and hence blamed the reductionism on the "*abundance of the material,*" referring to biographies of saints and the risk that "*the idea would have scandalized specialists of the genre*" without really telling us what is meant by "idea," "specialists" or "genre." [45] The charge that is leveled against Hammoudi (namely a-historicism) does not come from an exogenous model or methodology but instead from his own methodological pillars rendered explicit in the following words: "*We must rid ourselves of all assumptions of continuity-not that there is no continuity but that we must learn to see changes within continuity itself.*[46] The author tells us more about his methodological stance when he deems it *"unreasonable to continue to force dar al-mulk into the habitual typologies, such as the semi-traditional monarchy, neopatrimonialism, or some other neo-patriarchal form of government."*[47] In these lines Hammoudi does not operate as a continuity basher but rather as a continuity re-inventor. The only way one can perceive *dar al-Mulk* in its continuous form is through its definition as a field of power relationships mushroomed by the existence of the practices of service, gift exchange, and "sacred" terror.

Hammoudi's reliance on this ambivalence between tough and wimp tasks in the mystical path is anchored in a debatable and archaic view of the "sex of tasks." Since the beginning of time, we have been witnessing a gendered dichotomy between the male and the female to be followed in later times by that of the masculine and the feminine. One can recall here how Aristotle said in his *Historia Animalum* that men are more savage and more complete than women, who are more prone to compassion than the former. Even the attempt of Melford Spiros to show the triviality of biology in gendering our life has failed in an Israeli Kibbutz where boys were tougher than girls despite the fact that sex role identification was discouraged. The good old theory used by Hammoudi here is that withstanding the trials and tests of the mystical path and defying all the hardships of the way is the epitome of *masculinity* and that cooking and serving the master and showing shyness in his presence is the locus of *femininity*. Considering cooking and doing laundry feminine vices (They do not seem to be attributes at all for Hammoudi.) is a faith-based assumption that neither Foucault nor the prophetic model agree with. The fact that the prophet Muhammad (PBUH) cooked his food and milked his cows as the tradition narrates is never mentioned by Hammoudi, who rarely turns to any Islamic scripture to justify his position throughout this "deep and scholarly" work. We know that the mainstream standards of a "serious" academic study oblige the writer to treat prophetic narratives as an engineered display of power by "bloodthirsty" Arab womanizers, but our costly re-questioning of mainstream standards as channels of power allows us to see an emerging field of study totally comfortable with mixing academic "objectivity" with a passionate reverence for the sacred. If the Muslim "Nietzschean Superman" for the Sufis is the prophet Muhammad, how can we delve deeply into their way of using gendered symbols without even bothering to see the gendered symbols of their own model? If this sin of omission happened in American politics, we would discuss a foreign policy crisis without looking at the actions of the commander-in-chief, and certainly the likelihood of getting grants for this type of research is close to none.

With respect to faithfulness to the methodological premises of the Foucauldian paradigm by Hammoudi, the fact of positing social norms (cooking, being modest, and standing trial) in terms of sexual identification is definitely very "modern" for a postmodern author like Foucault. It is most probable that this really serious slip by a well-known and well-read anthropologist stems from his obsession with power rather than *subject-building* in the works of Foucault. To show clearly this point, let us give the floor to the "master" himself, who methodologically inspired our Moroccan Anthropologist:

"I would like to say, first of all, what has been the goal of my work during the last twenty years. It has not been to analyze the phenomena of power, nor to elaborate the foundations of such an analysis. My objective, instead, has been to create a

history of the different modes by which, in our culture, human beings are made subjects."[48]

What is interesting here in this testimony of Foucault, whom we safely assume understands his work better than anyone else, is the presence of two terms: *foundations* and *our culture*. With a farfetched irrationalism that I brought with me from the wonders of Africa, I can attribute some psychic powers to "Saint Foucault" here regarding the work of Hammoudi. By a linear extrapolation— a sensitivity that quantitative research helps us sharpen—of the word *foundations*, we can see Foucault telling anybody who wants to use his model to explore the *foundations of authoritarianism* hence of power: Hey, buddy, you are off track![49] We should not be deceived here by the fact the title of Hammoudi's book includes the process of making subjects out of human beings in the sense that it gives us an idea about the construction of both the master and his disciples. What we are saying here is that Hammoudi used the model designed by Foucault to "test" something for which this model was not designed, namely the foundations of power. When the possibility of a *woman saint* is ruled out—in defiance of the historical legacy of Moroccan female saints—

and when the access to the level of master is assumed to be the dream of every disciple, one can see how the obsession with power overrules any interest in inventing or reinventing the "subject." When Foucault mentions in his confession *"our culture,"* referring to the Western epistemological grounds of his work on power, he is using his psychic gifts to tell a potential user of his device to shake foundations that hardly speak Latin: Hey, buddy, you are again off track!

Brooke Olson clearly states in a review of Hammoudi's book that *"one problem of this work is that women are almost entirely absent from Hammoudi's analysis,"*[50] telling us how *"one wonders how he can speak of Sufi groups, both historically and in the present, without the mention of women as members of many of them."*[51] One can say here that Hammoudi did not talk about spaghetti either, and this is a more sarcastic way of asking the link between the omission of women saints and the model drawn by Hammoudi. In fact, when our anthropologist says that **inversion** is highly apparent in the master-disciple relationship because the disciple performs "feminine" tasks such as cooking and washing clothes, he is seeing that this negation of virility inverts the disciple's gender role. This loss of virility would make no sense (in a power relation context) without having the master (who is the holder of the "whip") embody the essence of the virility lost by the disciple. Furthermore, according to Hammoudi's thesis, the disciple has to regain "virility" again when he becomes a master. When a woman is the master, how can we interpret the loss of virility of her disciple in light of a loss of power? Wouldn't we be witnessing an empowerment of the feminine role via the master? This omission of the feminine here on the part of a Moroccan author leaves us with some implicit assumptions about gender in his work:

- Feminization is bad and inferior in status to virility. By setting an analogy between a master and a disciple on one side and a male and a female on the other side, Hammoudi sees a woman as a *man-to-be* in the same way he sees a disciple as a *master-to-be*.

- Cooking and washing clothes are *essentially* (in the sense of essentialism as a pathology) feminine and less valuable than manly tasks such as ruling and giving orders.

- Loss of power and submission is essentially feminine. This equation of loss of power with femininity is a male-made concept of *power over* rather than a more holistic one of *power with*.

- Ambiguity and ambivalence or the ability to be located between both genders is essentially bad: This stance misses the importance of androgyny as a resistance mechanism, as has been suggested by Foucault in his genealogical work on sexuality.

Neither Foucault nor the Sufis espouse those assumptions, which will be shown in the following lines. Hammoudi's account is still a prisoner of modernity as a philosophical construct in the sense of setting a male/female dichotomy and granting the latter a negative value. If loss of power is seen as feminine, aren't we here close to Freudian territory where "penis envy" is a national sport? When power is equated with domination we see that our Moroccan anthropologist is introducing us to a mystical "penis envy" where the she-disciple envies the penis as a symbol of power of the master and momentarily serves him until *she* deems it fit to become a "he" again. What about cases when the master is a female with no penis? What about when power is other than domination? What about when ambivalence (or androgyny, to use a term from literary theory) is a source of power rather than weakness?

We will try to understand these questions as we are exploring the Sufi framework that does not condemn dichotomization per se but uses it in accordance with a dogmatic belief in the separation of divine attributes into majestic (*jalal*) and aesthetic ones (*jamal*). The first ones have usually been associated with "masculine" attributes. Meanwhile, the second ones have been seen as representative of the "feminine" element of the divine. In the realm of the divine, those two categories are interchangeable and do not fall into a hierarchical taxonomy typical of the one used by Hammoudi. And in the rare instances where hierarchy (whether temporal or spatial) is introduced (such as in the *hadith*, where God tells us that his mercy precedes/supersedes his wrath) it is the feminine side that is highly valued. The divine attributes are divided in the Sufi terminology into majesty and beauty, wrath (*qahr*) and grace (*lutf*), or awe (*hayba*) and intimacy (*uns*). Visions of majestic attributes of God are linked to the concept of authority and tend to manifest generally in the form of the Sufi martyr's dictum '*I am the real*' (Hallaj), indicating an annihilation of the ego rather than a boasting contest (*mufakhara*) so dear to pre-Islamic Arabs. As far as the aesthetic attributes are concerned, the prophet Joseph comes to mind as the pinnacle of human beauty and also as a theophany of the divine. The verse about Joseph in the Koran tells us how Zulaykha told him to go out before the women of Egypt, when they started to gossip about her attraction to him, whereupon they cut their hands at the sight of his radiant face. Cutting the hand is definitely against the teachings of Islam and against the logic of utilitarianism, but don't we say that love is blind?

The same love should enter our explanatory paradigm when we are dealing with the issue of obedience in the master-disciple framework. In the same way some cold realists see a gentleman in love with a lady who gives her the famous belladonna glance as an ensnared poor victim loses his control, some social scientists remove the love variable from the master-disciple framework because they belong to a belief system fully loaded with slavery and modernist resentment of romantic attachment. If cutting the hands is mentioned and tolerated in the Koran *when love is present*, then what about the disciple fully in love with his or her master? Cutting the hand is painless when your heart is consumed with love, because pain is in the heart of the beholder. We have seen here that the Sufi framework has also its own majestic/aesthetic dichotomy, but it is more flexible in the sense that it allows for interchangeability and permutation—unlike the fixed one used by Hammoudi wherein the male character represents what is positive against a female character who represents all that is negative. We can also see that the archetypes of the masculine and the feminine used by Hammoudi are constructed by a patriarchal order. Meanwhile, for the Sufi framework, the feminine and masculine attributes are defined via revelation with respect to a God that transcends gender as a human construction. We are witnessing here not a negation of gender but rather its expansion. We have also seen that Hammoudi's account misses love as an explaining variable that somehow minimizes the role of coercive power. In a very interesting study of the distinctiveness of the master-disciple relationship from other social bonds such as the teacher-student, in the following words Joachim Wach introduces us eloquently to the necessity of taking into perspective love as an explaining variable.

> *"The teacher and student, united through a bond of work*
> *on a common task, form a series of links in which the student*
> *in his own proper time will also become a teacher. Conversely,*
> *the master and disciple in themselves represent the beginning*

and the end, a cosmos in itself; the disciple will never become
a master." [52]

He goes on to show that in this type of relationship the master gives him- or herself, while the teacher gives his or her knowledge. If the teacher lives through his or her work, the master survives in his or her disciples because the former provides a definite subject matter and the latter gives only stimulus. Moreover, the disciples fulfill three functions with respect to the master: They are the "representatives of mankind," they are companions, and finally they are proclaimers of the masterly teaching.

Foucault will not accept the essentialism that is characteristic of Hammoudi's treatment of cooking and washing the clothes of the master, since neither in the prophetic tradition nor in the Foucaultian paradigm do we find a *gendering* of domestic tasks. The Islamic attitude regarding domestic chores (in the Maliki School of Islamic jurisprudence adopted in Morocco) is that a woman is under no obligation to do the housework. The legal scholars define the marriage contract as a contract allowing all parties to enjoy themselves in that intimate relationship, rather than an agreement of servitude (*aqdu istimtaa*). In the words of

Ibn Hazm, one of the strictest literalist scholars, it is the duty of the husband to bring the food ready-cooked to his wife, and the legalists generally say that if an woman is one of the upper class, who are used to being served, it is the duty of the husband to provide her with a servant to look after him. When Aisha, the prophet's wife, was asked about the manner of the prophet (upon whom be blessings and peace) at home, she said that she used to be involved in the work of his family, repairing his clothes and shoes, and looking after his bed. Anthony Giddens was right in noticing a similarity between Foucault and Max Weber in the sense that both of them dealt with the separation of time and space as a mechanism of control. The division of tasks that Hammoudi engineered to express his fantasies about the feminization of a disciple would typically fall under the category of spatial manipulation and mainly *partitioning*, as Foucault described it. If we saw cooking as essentially masculine, we would be giving each gender an individualized location in order to facilitate our patriarchal hegemony and prevent any mixing between the two zones in the sense that we would be "gendering" a discourse about domestic tasks that has not been gendered before.

When it comes to attaching a value to the reified category named "the feminine," Hammoudi chooses to adopt a negative attitude by associating feminine tasks or attributes with passivity and servitude. What ontological tools were behind such a negative portrait? We can never claim to enter the author's mind, so we will embark on a journey of speculative reasoning on the basis of the references used. Is it Foucault and his gender blindness that explains this position? Or is it a deliberate attempt by the author to account for an existing patriarchal order within spheres of the Moroccan society? But if this is the case, what good does the deconstruction of a religious paradigm that is not typically Moroccan do for our interpretation?

It would be interesting to recall here that the framework of the master and disciple is not present in many societies that are famous for a female phobia. Furthermore, resistance against colonialism in Morocco has come mainly from the paradigm that is criticized by Hammoudi, which is that of the mystical brotherhoods. This historical fact does not seem to attract our author's interest, so to use the language of quantitative research, we see no correlation between the paradigm of master-disciple and authoritarianism, and we will skip the rational critique that would scold (figuratively speaking) Hammoudi for not introducing regressions and statistical tables. It is only when one is pragmatically absorbed into "physicality" that femininity is equated solely with domestic shores and lowering the gaze. In Sufi mysticism, the divine presence is presented in poetry as a feminine person like Layla. Thousands can quote stanzas from Majnun's poetry, describing his love for Layla as in these famous lines:

I pass by the house, the dwelling of Layla
And I kiss this wall and that wall.
It's not love of the dwelling that empassions my heart
But of she who dwells in the dwelling.

According to the famous Sufi scholar Ibn Arabi, "she" (*hiyya*) is a divine name like "he (*huwwa*) and the word for wisdom in Arabic is *feminine* (*hikma*). In his essay on the Indian Goddess Shakti, Frithjof Schuon expresses eloquently the complexity of the feminine when he says that *"on the one hand, one can oppose feminine sentimentality to masculine rationality-on the whole and without forgetting the relativity of things- but on the other hand, one also opposes to the reasoning of men the intuition of women; now is the gift of intuition, in superior women above all, that explains and justifies in large part the mystical promotion of the Feminine; it is consequently in this sense that the Haqiqah, esoteric knowledge, may appear as feminine."*[53] Each chapter in the Quran begins with the sentence "in the name of God, the Beneficent, the Merciful," and the two attributes beneficence and mercy come from the same root, which is a word for "womb" (*rahim*). Let us consider the reverent way in which Ibn Arabi describes his spiritual master, Fatima of Cordoba:

> *"I served as a disciple one of the lovers of God, a Gnostic, a lady of Seville called Fatimah bint Ibn al-Muthanna of Cordova [...] with my own hands I built for her a hut of reeds as high as she, in which she lived until she died. She used to say to me 'I am your spiritual mother and the light of your earthly mother."*[54]

What we can learn from this passage is that sainthood can be motherhood and can be feminine, which renders any description of feminization as a loss of power or virility awkward. In a very interesting article incredibly similar to Hammoudi's ideas, Margaret Malamud talks about the act of transmitting the *dhikr* as the injection of semen into the disciple but goes on to remind us that *"gender imagery in Sufi texts symbolizes more than engendering and paternal authority[...]Sheikhs are also described as mothers."* [55] Malamud continues her explanation of the concept of duality when she tells us that spiritual masters are both fathers and mothers in that they give a new life to their disciples in the same way semen is a new bodily life and that in the meantime they nurture their offspring using the analogy of breastfeeding. As a matter of fact, the famous Sufi scholar Sadr al-Din Qunawi said while describing his learning process: *"I have drunk from the breasts of two mothers."*

Foucault never talked about power without resistance, so the feminization of the disciple could have been a form of resistance rather than a loss of power if understood in light of an emerging literature on androgyny. The potential of androgyny to trouble the binary oppositions and go beyond boundaries was mentioned by Linda Stewart when she wrote:

> *"To define "androgyny" as a gender identity which troubles-by conflating, confusing and even erasing-traditional gender categories enables a reading of such ambiguously gendered*

figures as Findley's Lucy and King's Coyote/Four Old Indians as subversive not only of sexism/heterosexism, but of authoritarian regimes, within which sexism and heterosexism operate, more generally. Redefinition of 'androgyny' as a trope which figures refusal to conform to hierarchical binary oppositions of all sorts extends the insights of contemporary work in gender studies to construct a figure that performs resistance to authoritarianism in its multiple social, religious, political and economic manifestations." 56

Men are females in the womb of their mother, and as they gradually grow their femininity gives way to their masculinity until they reach the age of forty, when they regain it to reach full androgyny. This chronological order described by Jung and Levinson sends us back to the symbolic meaning of forty in prophecy and spiritual evolution as if spiritual achievement and androgyny are causally correlated. Ibn Arabi has also mentioned that when he saw in the union of the male and the female an achievement of the holistic union with the divine. This ambiguity is described by the poet al-Mutanabi, who wrote a verse in which he tells us about the sun being feminine in the Arabic language and the moon being masculine:

> *Were Women as I have described,*
> *Women would be superior to men.*
> *Femininity is no defect in the sun,*
> *Nor should the moon be proud of masculinity*

We can see here that androgyny offers us numerous ways of resistance by questioning existing dichotomies and extracting the feminine element in masculine disciples, or even as a form of empowering through the garment of sainthood, a discourse of femininity in face of the hegemonic presence of the patriarchal discourse. Sometimes gender reversal is only a means to an end on the spiritual path, as is the case with this story of the Moroccan saint Abu Yi'zza, whose companion got married and his wife asked him about a female slave, which he could not afford. Abu Yi'zza dressed as a female slave and served the couple for an entire year until she found out about it and she swore that she would do the work herself.

Conclusion

We have seen in this paper that the shadow of anthropology haunts this account of mystical brotherhood and hence puts some bias in it since Hammoudi favors institutional knowledge and espouses a colonialist view of Sufism based on an ignorance of the dimension of love and charisma present in the Sufi paradigm. We deconstructed the field of anthropology used by Hammoudi to show how the authoritarianism that he found in the mystical framework might come from his discipline.

We have used a paradigm of a Moroccan philosopher (Taha Abderrahmane) to show how it is helpful to subject any interpretation of a phenomenon to the ontology that produced it. We proceeded to some linguistic analysis of the terminology used in Sufism, and we have shown how the introduction of the Arabic language helps us dispel the myth of coercion behind what seems to be an exercise of blind submission by the disciples. The idea of creed or faith helps us look at the intention of different actors and thus makes us see that a political party dressed in the suit of mysticism does not make it mystical. Certain texts from the prophetic narrations were used here to find a genealogical legitimacy for the practices in Sufism that might be seen as hegemonic. Hence, the act of allegiance is linked with a divine covenant that transcends space and time. By depriving the covenant of its human form, we move to a less coercive form of power.

We analyzed also the framework of Michel Foucault to see whether Hammoudi respected it in his main assumptions, and we have found that by categorizing domestic chores in the feminine, the Moroccan anthropologist went against one of the main pillars of Foucault. The narrative in this book is a-historical against the genealogical nature of the Foucauldian approach. The fact that Hammoudi ignores the lives of women saints makes us wonder how patriarchal power is then explained as a product of mysticism. We have also used the findings of queer theory to see gender ambivalence not as a loss of masculinity and power but rather as a potential resistance against fixed identities. Moreover, we have shown how this androgyny is an offspring of the mystical treatment of divine names. We have also seen how the traditional mystical initiation deals with power and politics in the same way as quantum politics by questioning the separation of object and subject and by focusing on relations rather than persons. Relational accounts are in a continual redefinition of identities and therefore the Sufi framework of today cannot be judged only through an analysis of previous Sufi models. The main finding of this work ironically borrows the same road followed by Hammoudi in that it looks at foundations. The idea that the master-disciple framework is a cultural ancestor to authoritarianism was deconstructed by showing how the use and misuse of Foucault and the omission of authentic and important variables such as love and language carry the seeds of authoritarianism. We have used education as well to see how the analysis of this relationship between the master and the disciple follows the law of traditional learning and cannot be judged according to the standards of modern academia. This might lead us to ask ourselves in turn, Can a paper that is written with traditional canons have a chance of passing through the filters of modern academia?

Endnotes

[1] See an article by Moulay Hicham in *L'intelligent* (08/09/2001) in which he responds to his critics.

[2] This point is not to be taken literally. A basic course in linguistics teaches us that when you call someone "a cow" you are not referring to that milky animal that vegetarians dislike. "*I do not have an audience*" means here that being published and earning ovations is not my goal in life, as is the case with some scholars.

[3] Ernest, Carl W, "The Study of Religion and the Study of Islam", unc.edu/~cernst/study.html

[4] The question of whether this Amazon.com excerpt is authoritative can never be solved; therefore, as a writer I can grant whomever I want whatever I want. An alternative answer would be that in age of internet, the most widely visited site in the book business is the Amazon.

[5] Munson, Henry. *Religion and Power in Morocco*, Yale University Press: New Haven, 1993, p.185.

[6] ibid, p.185

[7] Nancy, Fraser, "Michel Foucault: A 'Young Conservative'?" *Ethics*, Vol.96, n.1 (1985).

[8] David, Price, "Anthropologists as Spies" *The Nation*, November 20 2000, p.24.

[9] ibid, p.25

[10] Vincent, Cornell, *Realm of The Saint: Power and Authority in Moroccan Sufism*, Austin: University of Texas Press, 1998, p.93.

[11] Robert Lee Hotz, "High Priests of the Unknown," *Los Angeles Times Magazine*, December 2, 2001.

[12] Constance, Classen, "Other Ways to Wisdom: Learning Through The Senses Across Cultures," *Learning, Knowledge and Cultural Context*, Linda King, Kluwer Academic Publishers, 1999, p.271.

[13] Since we assume that Arabic is a revealed rather than a consensual language, it is immune from people's power. God's omnipotent positive power is implicitly presented in the image.

[14] Hammoudi, Abdellah, *Master and Disciple: The Cultural Foundations of Moroccan Authoritarianism*, The University of Chicago Press: Chicago, 1997, p.vii.

[15] Hammoudi, p.xxi

[16] Hammoudi, p.5

[17] Hammoudi, p.1

[18] Hammoudi, p.xix

[19] Di Zerega, Gus, in *Quantum Politics: Applying Quantum theory to Political Phenomena*, Becker, Theodore, Praeger: NY, 1991, p.84.

[20] Voll, John, "Sultans, Saints, and Presidents," *Islam, Democracy, and the State in North Africa*, John Entelis, Bloomington: Indiana University Press, 1997, p.4.

[21] Hammoudi, p.141

[22] The hadith of Gabriel, Muslim, Iman 1; Bukhari, Iman 37; MM 5-6

23 Murata, Sachicko and Chittick, William, *The Vision of Islam*, Paragon House: St.Paul, 1994, p.xxxiii.

24 Hammoudi, ibid, p.85

25 Hammoudi, ibid, p.134

26 Murata and Chittick, ibid, p.51

27 Armstrong, Karen, Muhammad, p.77.

28 Armstrong, ibid, p.77

29 An alternative explanation is the evolutionary thesis saying that our fathers were apes. I am speaking in light of what the author believes, namely that Adam is our father. Otherwise, the monkeys' thesis is not the only explanation since there is also coincidence and aliens…

30 Hammoudi., ibid, p.93

31 Munson, Henry, op cited, p.4

32 Munson, op cited, p.6

33 Munson, op cited, p.6

34 Munson, op cited, p.19

35 Munson, op cited, p.24

36 Winch, Peter in *Understanding and Social Inquiry*, Dallmayr, Fred and McCarthy A.Thomas, University of Notre Dame: London, 1977, p.180.

37 Wei-Ming, Tu, Confucian Thought: Selfhood as Creative Transformation, Albany, NY: SUNY Press, 1985, p.21.

38 Di Zerega, op cited, p.92

[39] *Prophetic Charisma: The Psychology of Revolutionary Religious Personalities,* NY: Syracuse University Press, 1997.

[40] I am using the way Derrida plays with *difference* and *differance'* in the case of *maani* and *m'aani*.

[41] Hammoudi, op.cited, p.139

[42] Bayman, Henry, *The Station of No Station,* Berkley: North Atlantic Books, 2001, p.199.

[43] Olson, Brooke. *The Journal of Religion,* Vol 79, No. 3, July 1999, p.506.

[44] Hammoudi, Abdellah, "The Reinvention of Dar al-Mulk: The Moroccan Political System and Its Legitimation," *In the Shadow of the Sultan,* Rahma Bourqia & Susan Miller, Harvard University Press, 1999.

[45] Bourqia, Rahma ,op cited, p.143

[46] Bourquia, Rahma, op cited, p.169

[47] Bourquia, Rahma, op cited, p.170

[48] Foucault, M., *The Subject and Power: After word to 'Michel Foucault, Beyond Structuralism and Hermeneutics,'* The Harvester Press: 1982, p.208.

[49] When informal and "street language" is inserted in an essay haunted by scholarly formalism, it becomes a voluntary rhetorical tool with two main goals: bridging the gap at a linguistic level between what is formal and informal, elitist and popular, white and indigenous on the one hand; and questioning the censorship of "fun," as I have come to understand it in modern and often "frigid" academia on the other hand. Given the fact that I show a respectable amount of familiarity with "publishable" English, the use of "non-presentable" expressions is to be understood as a linguistic aphrodisiac for academic writing rather than a need

on my part to nourish the account of the English Language Institute.

[50] Olson, Brooke, op cited, p.506

[51] Olson, Brooke, op cited, p.506

[52] Wach, Joachim, "Master And Disciple: Two Religio-Sociological Studies," *The Journal of Religion* 42, No.1, January 1962, p.2 .

[53] Schuon, Frithjof, *Roots of the Human Condition*, Bloomington: World Wisdom Books, 1991, pp.29-45

[54] Ibn Arabi, *Sufis of Andalusia*, Gloucestershire: Beshara publications, 1988, pp.25-26

[55] Malamud, Margaret, "Gender and Spiritual Fashioning: The Master-Disciple Relationship in Classical Sufism," *Journal of the American Academy of Religion*, Spring 1996, Vol LXIV, No.1, p.97.

[56] Linda Lamont-Stewart, "Androgyny as Resistance to Authoritarianism in Two Postmodern Canadian Novels," *Mosaic*, 30/3, September 1997, p.129.

Bibliography

Books

Munson, Henry. *Religion and the Power in Morocco.* Yale University Press, New Haven, 1993.

Constance, Classen. *Other Ways to Wisdom: Learning Through the Senses Across Cultures – Learning, Knowledge and Cultural Context.* Linda King, Kluwer Academic Publishers, 1999.

Hammoudi, Abdellah. *Master and Disciple: The Cultural Foundations of Moroccan Authoritarianism.* The University of Chicago Press, Chicago, 1997.

Hammoudi, Abdellah. *The Reinvention of Dar Al-Mulk: The Moroccan Political System and Its Legitimating – In the Shadow of the Sultan.* Rahma Bourqia and Susan Miller, Harvard University Press, 1999.

Vincent, Cornell. *Realm of the Saint: Power and Authority in Moroccan Sufism.* University of Texas Press, Austin, 1998.

Voll, John. *Sultans, Saints, and Presidents, Islam, Democracy and the State in North Africa.* John Entelis, Bloomington, Indiana University Press, 1997.

Winch, Peter in *Understanding and Social Inquiry*. Dallmayr, Fred and McCarthy. A. Thomas (ed). University of Notre Dame, London, 1997.

Wei-Ming, Tu. *Confucian Thought: Selfhood as Creative Transformation*. SUNY Press, Albany, New York, 1985.

Bayman, Henry. *The Station of No Station*. North Atlantic Books, Berkley, 2001.

M., Foucault. *The Subject and Power: Afterword to Michael Foucault, Beyond Structuralalism and Hermeneutics*. Harvard University Press, 1982.

Schuon, Frithjof. *Roots of the Human Condition*. World Wisdom Books, Bloombington, 1991.

Ibn Arabi. *Sufism of Andalusia*. Beshara Publications, Gloucestershrine, 1988.

Schimmel, Annemarie. *Mystical Dimensions of Islam*. University of North Carolina Press, 1996.

Moinuddin Chishti, Hakim. *The Book of Sufi Healing*. Inner Traditions International, 1991.

O'Toole, John and Khemir Nancer. *The Wisdom of Islam*. Abbeville Press, 1996.

Frager, Robert. *Heart, Self and Soul: A Sufi Approach to Growth, Balance and Harmony*. Theosophical Publishing House, 1999.

Shah, Idries. *Knowing How to Know: A Practical Philosophy in the Sufi Tradition*. Octagon Press, 2000.

Journal Articles

Fraser, Nancy. *Michel Foucault: A Young Conservative?* Ethics, Vol. 96, No. 1 (1985)

Lee Hotz, Robert. *High Priests of the Unknown.* Los Angeles Times Magazine, December 2, 2001.

Becker, Theodore. *Di Zerega Gus in Quantum Politics: Applying Quantum Theory to Political Phenomena.* Praeger, New York, 1991.

Murata, Sachicko and Chittick, William. *The Vision of Islam.* Paragon House, St. Paul, 1994.

Oaks, Len. *Prophetic Charisma: The Psychology of Revolutionary Religious Personalities.* Syracuse University Press, New York, 1997.

Master and Disciple book review. Olson, Brooke. The Journal of Religion, Vol. 79, July 1999.

Wash, Joachaim. *Master and Disciple: Two Religio-Sociological Studies.* The Journal of Religion 42, No. 1, January 1962.

Lamont-Stewart, Linda. *Androgyny as Resistance to Authoritarianism in Two Postmodern Canadian Novels.* Mosaic, 30/3, September 1997.

Malamud, Margaret. *Gender and Spiritual Fashioning: Master-Disciple Relationship in Classical Sufism.* Journal of the American Academy of Religion, Vol. LXIV, No. 1, 1996.

Newspaper Articles

Price, David. *Anthropologists as Spies.* The Nation, November 20, 2000.

Moulay Hisham, L'intelligent. August 9, 2001.

Electronic Resources

Ernest, Carl W. *The Study of Religion and the Study of Islam.* www.unc.edu/~cernst/study.html.

About the Author

Abdelilah Bouasria left Morocco in 1993 with a DEUG in economics from Mohamed V University in Rabat to Canada where he earned his B.com from McGill University in Montreal. He went then to England where he obtained his MA in international relations at Sussex University in Brighton. He came to American University in Washington DC for a second MA in political science and he is finishing there his PhD in comparative politics with a focus on Islam and democracy as well as Sufism in Morocco. He has several publications in Arabic, French and English. He resides in Monterey, California where he teaches Arabic at the Defense Language Institute in Monterey. He is the author of *Mamlakatul Qaht* (Royaume de La Soif), Nadacom, Rabat 2006.